"This is absolutely wonderful."
Donna Robinson, Attorney; Author, *No Kiss Goodbye*

"I absolutely love this book. As a minister, I would love to have this book on my bookshelf. It is a fantastic resource of sermon illustrations and inspirational thoughts."
Rev. Tony Adams, Ordained Bishop in the Church of God (Cleveland); Pastor of New Vision Church, Holland, Michigan; Faculty member at Cornerstone University; Author, *Shepherd Leadership: A Path Forward*

"You tell these stories very cleanly and simply, and I think that gives them strength."
Tod Schneider, Poet; Author, *The Lost Wink*

"This is a fantastic concept and I think your short stories will hit the spot with all kinds of people. I found your work easy to read, easy to understand, and relevant."
Lenny Banks, Author, *Time and Tide: At the Rock*

"[I] found the short passages to be quite inspirational and encouraging. They are relevant and written from the heart of one who truly understands the challenges of real life."
James Revoir, Author, *Priceless Stones*

"Your work is really interesting and a terrific concept of 'fill in the blanks'!"
Anya Maisey, Author, *The Word According to Dog*

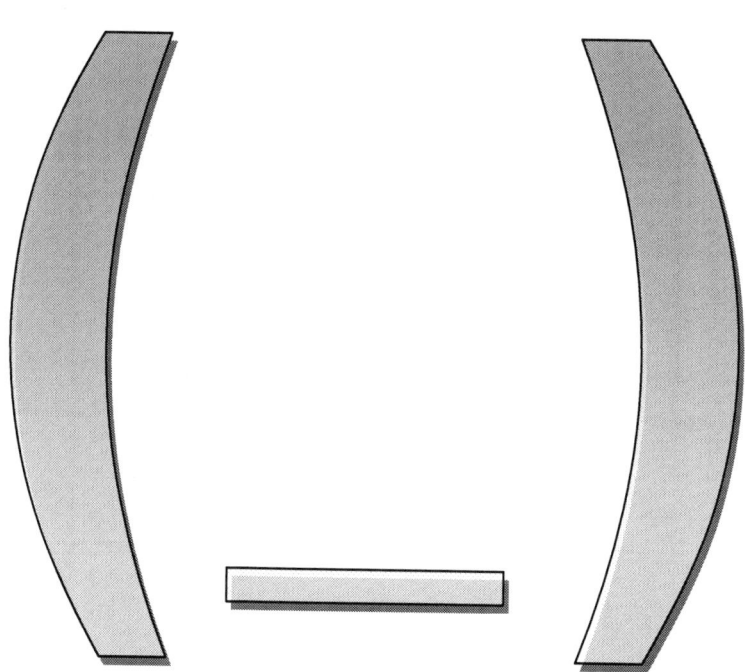

Fill In The Blank
Vol. 1

Inspiring Truths in a Busy World

JASON M. FRAZIER

Revised and Expanded

Published by CreateSpace and Amazon.com
Printed in the United States of America

First Edition: 2012
Revised and Expanded Second Edition: 2014

Unless otherwise noted, Scripture quotations are taken from the New International Version of the Holy Bible available for free on www.BibleGateway.com .

For more information, visit **www.FillintheBlank.me** or e-mail **FillintheBlankBook@gmail.com**

Logo, concept, book design, and website by Jason M. Frazier

Editor: Monica S. Gillespie

ISBN-10:1497529891
ISBN-13:978-1497529892

DEDICATIONS

To my Lord and Savior Jesus Christ

To my wife

To my children

CONTENTS

Introduction

I was getting coffee in the break room at my office when a coworker walked up to me. He told me about visiting a church the past weekend and hearing the story of Jonah, complete with the part of Jonah being vomited up on the beach. This is a very familiar story to most people because it makes the rounds in Sunday school lessons for children quite frequently.

Being very acquainted with the story, I told him, "You know, God was doing Jonah a favor that day." My friend looked puzzled by my comment.

I said, "Well, we always read that story with the end of it in mind, but Jonah did not know how the story would unfold. If you want to get down to it, he was the worst missionary ever. First, he argued with God so God would not make him go to Nineveh.

"Second, when God insisted, Jonah got on a boat headed in the wrong direction.

"Third, when the storm arose and threatened to destroy the boat, Jonah chose suicide rather than obedience. He did not know that God had prepared a fish to be his vessel back to the shore. He thought he would die and that would be the end of his mission to Nineveh.

"Fourth, it was only inside the belly of the whale that he submitted to God's will.

"Fifth, when he did go to Nineveh, he did not tell them what to do to be saved; he only told them that God was going to destroy them. He offered no plan of salvation or deliverance.

"Finally, after he preached the message and was disappointed when God did not destroy Nineveh, he complained that God was too forgiving! He was, by far, the worst missionary ever!"

My friend had not heard this version of Jonah at church that past Sunday. Then I repeated, "But God did Jonah a tremendous favor that day." My friend replied, "And what was that?"

"There were two ways out of that fish: the front and the back. God could have let Jonah be fully digested and make his way out the back... or he could get Jonah out through the front via an 'express lane.' Trust me, God did Jonah a favor."

Laughing at this point, my friend said, "In all the times I have heard that story, I have never heard it put that way. You have got to write this stuff down. Write these stories with your perspective and give some sort of motivational or inspirational thoughts with them."

You, dear reader, hold in your hand the fruit of that labor. This book is merely volume one of a forthcoming, multi-volume set of inspirational stories and challenges to you, the reader.

The original version of each chapter came from a one-page article that I e-mailed out to subscribers. I kept it to one-page specifically so my subscribers could read these articles in three minutes or less. Most of them ended with questions and a challenge to mentally "fill in the blank." However, some readers of the first edition requested that I release an updated edition with actual blanks so they can write in their copies. Also, the request came to expand the chapters, since I was no longer under the one-page limitation to e-mail subscribers in the book.

Lastly, I would like to take this opportunity to mention the many people to whom I owe a tremendous debt of gratitude:

- My wife, Angela: You are a constant source of encouragement to me. You believed in me, have supported my goals, and continue to push me to excel.

- My children: You had to share me with this project, but you believed in it and were excited to see your dad become an author. I am so thankful for your love and admiration. I hope the life lessons contained in this book will help you develop into followers of Christ.

- My friend, Emile: As you well know, you were the coworker in the break room who challenged me to write this book, and served as my editor for the first edition. This project would have never seen the light of day if it were not for you. You had the vision for this and kept pushing me to stretch my thinking. You are a good friend and a fantastic photographer. May both of our dream jobs come true.

- My friend, Monica: You have been a great supporter, promoter, and editor of this revised edition. I appreciate your advice. Thank you for all you have done for this version to be greater than the first.

- My dad, Dr. Donald M. Frazier: You were my very first pastor and mentor. You helped me learn to love God's word and develop the art of storytelling. I am grateful for your tutelage and investment.

- My dearly departed mother, Abbie Frazier: I am so grateful for the life lessons you instilled in me of kindness, generosity, gentleness, patience, and long-suffering. I was never a perfect son, yet you loved me and believed in me.
- My mentors in ministry, as well as many godly men who were models for me to follow: Though not an exhaustive list, these men include Bill Splawn, Eugene Perrault, Dick Herman, Brady Durling, Dr. Gaylan Claunch, Scott Wilson, Dr. Gene Brown. Dr. LeRoy Bartel, Eugene Reiszner, Mike Reiszner, Steve Owens, Larry Allgood, Eugene McBride, Douglas Raine, Ray Guinn, David Kent, my professors at Southwestern Assemblies of God University, my professors at Liberty Baptist Theological Seminary, and many others.

Gold

There are times in our lives where we go through testing. We face a discouraging diagnosis at the Doctor's office. We get demoted at work because of something outside our control. We are suckered into an investment that was a sure thing, only to realize it was a waste of time and resources.

Sometimes we feel like we are wandering in the wilderness, not sure of where we are headed or what is around the next corner. The uncertainty is tormenting. When we pray, it can feel like our prayers are bouncing back off the clouds at us.

The fact is that we all go through times of trials and tests. No one is immune or exempt from them. Some tests are physical where our health is being attacked. Some are financial where a gigantic debt has been created and we have to figure out how we will rebound. Some tests are personal where we experience a breakdown in a close relationship. Some are emotional where we have been carrying a tremendous weight on our shoulders that we cannot seem to bear anymore. Maybe it is a spiritual conflict that we have been going through and we feel like we are groping in the dark.

In the days of the Old Testament, the prophet Isaiah shared God's words to His people Israel regarding this issue. God was upset with their stubbornness and hard hearts. God told them that He would delay His wrath against them for their many sins and evildoing. His desire was not to destroy them, but to perfect them. God illustrated that by saying, "See, I have refined you, though not as silver; I have tested you in the furnace of affliction."[1]

Since God relates to testing and trials to the process of refining gold and silver, let us take a look at that process. A goldsmith takes gold and begins to melt it in the furnace. He adds harsh elements that force the gold to separate from the impurities. As the heat is turned up, the impurities rise to the surface.

The goldsmith scoops off the impurities and allows the gold to cool. He repeats this process by increasing the heat, removing the impurities, and allowing the gold to cool down. The more he does this, the purer the gold becomes. The most valuable type is 24-karat gold which is one-hundred percent gold with no impurities. Because it is so pure, it is very pliable and flexible. It can mold into any shape in the hands of the goldsmith.

The hard part for us is going through the fire. It can be very painful. It can be very lonely. In one translation of the Bible, there are over a dozen references to God refining His people like gold or silver. He is not interested in our lives being filled with impurities that weigh us down. His purpose is to refine us and conform us more and more into the likeness that He had planned all along.

Purity is a high commodity in our culture. We would not want our food or drinks loaded down with fillers that are not what we are paying for. We would not want our gasoline to be *mostly* gas. We would not want our shampoo and body wash to include a percentage of dirt and grime. Why do we not make the same connection to our personal lives?

Fill in the Blank: What areas of your life are being tested right now? _____

_____

_____

_____

Determine right now that you will come through these trials refined as pure gold. Do not *ever* forget that these trials are temporary. The heat will be turned down. The trial will end. The difficulties will pass. Just make sure you let the Master Refiner do His job and let those impurities in your life get scooped away. This is how you become what He wants you to be.

Exit

If you ever went to Sunday school as a child, you undoubtedly heard the story of Jonah. He was what we call "The Reluctant Prophet." God had told him to share a message with a very evil city, Nineveh. The ruins of that town today are in northern Iraq.

However, Jonah did not want to go there. Instead he boarded a boat headed from Joppa in Israel to Tarshish. The story doesn't tell us why he ran away, but it does provide an interesting statement. "Jonah ran away from the LORD. . ."[1]

In the Hebrew, it reads, "But Jonah stood up to run away from the face of the LORD. . ." What Jonah was doing ended up being quite impossible.

Tarshish was not quite in the opposite direction, but it definitely was not in the *right* direction.

When a terrible storm hit the Mediterranean Sea, Jonah confessed that God had sent the storm because he refused to obey. While these sailors feared for their lives, Jonah offered the only suitable solution he could think up: they should kill him.

I'm sure your Sunday School Teacher candy-coated that part. Telling children that a Bible character was trying to commit suicide instead of obeying God's command just would not sit well with parents after church.

Jonah told the sailors to throw him overboard during a very violent storm. He had no absolutely idea that God had prepared a great fish to swallow him and get him back to the shore. In Jonah's mind, *suicide* was a better solution than *submission*.

Once inside the fish, Jonah realized the error of his ways. Digestion was not as appealing to him as drowning. As it is with us many times, we do not see how foolish a path we have chosen until we are already in the belly of a fish, the bottom of a pit, or at the brink of ruin.

God left Jonah inside that fish for seventy-two hours. Three very long days. Jonah finally submitted to God, vowed to go to Nineveh, and preach the message that God had given him.

However, there remained one final dilemma for Jonah. How do you get a man out of the stomach of a fish? There were two exits: the front or the back. The back way would surely kill Jonah. If it did not, he probably would wish that it had. So God was gracious and allowed the fish to vomit Jonah out onto the shore.

There are times in our lives when we know what we should do, yet we do anything *but* that thing. We choose our own wisdom above God's. We choose our way, our will, and our plan. We think and act as if we know better than God. It is as if God's plan is one way, but there is another plan – our plan – that is just as good. Yet for a person who chooses to be a Christian, this idea will not work.

God's plan is Plan A. It is the best plan. It is the plan where we usually do not end up being eaten by something. If you insist on doing your own thing, making your own way, and ignoring God's desired destiny for your life, I wish you the best. Hopefully the fate of others who have done just that and did not live to tell about it will not be your fate. However, you would be hard-pressed to pick up the Bible and find an exception.

Ask yourself this question: "Areas of my life that I know I am not doing what God wants me to do are:

_____

_____

_____

_____."

Figure out what those are, find out what God wants you to do, and pray that God gives you a clean exit.

Disobedience leads to digestion.

Finish

Derek Redmond. You might remember him as the Olympic runner in 1992 that, during the race of his life, pulled his hamstring.[1] He was favored to win. In fact, he was winning the race at the time. He was supposed to be a super-athlete that would shatter records.

When he heard the pop in his leg, he felt tremendous pain. He tried to hop on one leg, but he knew in his mind what had happened. His body hit the track, lame. Paramedics rushed to his side. But he would not go with them. He somehow managed to get back up and stand on his good leg.

You could see this look on his face of unbearable disappointment. He had let everybody down: himself, his coach, and his parents.

Most people assumed that he would hobble off the track and go into the ambulance under his own power. The race was, after all, over. It had been won by an American, Steve Lewis. But that is when something even more bizarre happened. Derek started hobbling down the track towards the finish line. He winced in pain with every hop. He still had 175 meters to go. That is a long way to go on one leg.

I watched this event live on TV as an older man leapt out of the bleachers to run after him. Initially, security tried to detain him, but he shrugged them off. He ran right up to Derek and put his arm around him. He did not try to stop him from running the race. He knew that it was something Derek had to do for himself. Derek had resolved to cross the finish line whether he walked or crawled. He had come to the Olympics to finish.

Derek with his father, walking arm in arm, crossed the finish line to the sound of 65,000 people cheering, crying and clapping. It was a monumental experience for sports. One writer called it the "triumph of the human spirit."[2]

What you may not know is that this was not the first heartbreak for Derek Redmond. He was only ten minutes away from running in the 1988 Olympics before he suffered an Achilles tendon injury. Five surgeries later, he was back in the fight.

Derek simply did not know the meaning of the word "quit." That is why he got up. That is why he would not be denied. After his injury in Barcelona in 1992, it was not about medals anymore. It was all about finishing the race.

I was a sophomore in college and was ready to drop out and come home. As I spoke with my dad on the phone, he and my mom were very supportive of me and listened to my concerns. After letting me finish, my dad said, "Jason, everybody starts off the race strong. But it is not how you start that matters. It is how you finish. You are a 'finisher.' I know you can do it. Just finish the race. We will finish strong together." Once a week, I would get a letter or card of encouragement from my parents. They put their arms around me emotionally and helped me cross the finish line.

Fill in the Blank: "Some areas of my life that I need to be a 'finisher' in are _____

_____

_____

and I am headed for the goal. The finish line may be out of sight, but I will not be denied. I choose to overcome any obstacles or hardships in my way. I have come to finish. *I will not be denied*."

Pink

Anyone who has ever opened a paycheck, letter from their employer or bill knows that pink is not a good color to see. Just the mere sight of it can strike fear in the heart of anyone. I wondered why the color pink was used in these instances.

Supposedly, employment applications and termination notices had to be completed in triplicate.[1] The middle copy, the pink one, was given to the employee as theirs. So when a person was terminated, they received the pink slip. However, I wondered if there was a deeper psychology behind it.

I discovered that pink is the color associated with passiveness, sensitivity, and empathy.[2] Therefore, it's like the paper is saying to you, "We know this is bad news, but remain calm. We still like you as a human being."

I am a "silver lining" kind of person in many instances. I understand that getting a pink slip is a tough pill to swallow. However, a radio preacher named C.M. Ward said something along the lines of: "Nothing helps you make up your mind like getting fired." I can attest to that fact.

I was enjoying a great job with a great boss. I loved every minute of it. But I had a nagging feeling in my gut that something substantial was about to happen. I felt like I would not be there much longer. I did not want to accept that, so I worked even harder showing my commitment to the organization and leadership. In the end, it was not enough.

It was not about performance. It was about the budget. I was given sixty days' notice to find other employment. C.M. Ward's quote came screaming back at me. I could not stay there even if I wanted to. God had been preparing me for a transition and I was right at the start of it.

Throughout those sixty days, I saw God perform some amazing miracles for new employment, new housing, moving bills being paid, and so many other blessings. God had paved the way for me to step into a new company and a new role.

You see, a pink slip does not have to be a bad thing. It can be God's way of getting you out of where you are so He can take you to where He wants you to be. If you ever get handed the proverbial pink slip, just whisper a prayer of thanks to God. With God at the helm, you never sail into uncharted waters.

Fill in the Blanks: Are you prone to fear and anxiety?

_____

Do you find yourself worrying about a lot of things, whether those things are big or small? _____

_____

What are things you find yourself worrying about?

_____

_____

_____

If you got a pink slip today, would you react passively or would you start attacking coworkers with your stapler?

_____

Take a deep breath, and let God do what He does best: take care of you.

Fruit

Have you ever noticed that fruit does not grow near the shelter of the tree trunk?

I have never come across any fruit in God's creation where the fruit actually grows at the base of the tree. If you were to walk through the forest one day, you would not see any apples, oranges, kiwi, or lemons growing at the tree trunk.

However, what you will see in nature is that fruit grows *away* from the shelter of the tree trunk. It hangs out there on the end of the branch being pelted by rain, whipped around by gusting winds and scorched by the sun. The fruit is completely exposed to all of the elements that could easily destroy it. Yet out on the farthest parts of the branches, fruit grows. Even more, it does not just grow; it flourishes.

Each person is created to bear fruit. In fact, mankind was commanded to "Be fruitful. . ." several times in the Bible.[1] Whatever the dream is inside your heart, it is the fruit that you were created to bring into this world. When you are doing what you were created to do, the storms in your life cannot keep you from being fruitful.

If you want to truly bear fruit in your life, just like in nature, *you have to be willing to go out on a limb.* Think about that last sentence for a minute. Read it again. If you want to be fruitful, *you have to go out on a limb.*

If you are not in a place to do that, then it might be time. If you dream about doing something other than what you are doing right now, then seriously assess where you are and where you want to be.

The right seeds have already been planted in your heart. However, you have to water those seeds. You need to cultivate the soil. This means that you need to make sure your surroundings are conducive to bringing this fruit into your life. Sometimes you need to prune some things out of your life to make way for the right things to come in.

When I wanted to learn how to play the guitar, I surrounded myself with people who already knew how to play. I watched their hands as they moved effortlessly up and down the fret board. I watched how they alternated strings when they were finger picking. I intently studied and learned strum patterns, chord charts, and tablature until I went from a guitar student to a guitar player. How did it happen? I nourished the seed until fruit began to come forth.

When the seed is watered, cultivated, nourished, and has room to grow, the fruit will come. It will come forth because all of the right elements are in place. It will not feel like work; it will be completely natural. When you get to the place where you are operating in your strengths and see the results, you will be fulfilled.

Fill in the Blank: What is the fruit of which you dream, and what do you need to do today to start living that dream?_____

_____

_____

_____

_____

_____

Weather

You probably have a favorite season which is usually attached to some treasured memories. For my kids, their favorite season is summer because of the break from school, sleeping late, ice cream, parties, concerts, and day-time trips to the mall.

For me, it is autumn. I guess it could be the cool morning air and the pleasant temperatures in the afternoon that are not too warm. To me, it is just the perfect season. I think I am actually happier that time of year.

Have you ever noticed that your mood can be affected by the weather? On hot and sunny days, my kids seem extra-energetic. They crave snow cones, hot dogs, fireworks, and a trip to the neighborhood pool. On cold days, we may be a little more sluggish. We want soup, the smell of treated wood in the fireplace, and a huge, cozy blanket covering us while we sit on the couch to our favorite seasonal movie.

Then there are the storms. I am not just talking about rain. I am talking about storms with thunder that shakes the house and lightning that illuminates the blackest of nights. Weather like that can make you feel small and powerless.

The reason is that your mood is often affected by your circumstances. When things are going good, you are happy. When things are going bad, you are not happy. A rough time at home, with your finances, with your boss, or with your kids can create a very bad mood. It is unsettling. It is unnerving.

Living in this way is akin to sailing in the ocean. The circumstances in your life will hit the boat regardless. Storms will arise. But the direction the boat is turned makes all the difference in the world. If it is turned parallel to the waves, it will surely capsize and be destroyed.

You will not be able to weather the storm.

However, if you choose to turn the rudder, sail your boat towards the waves, and confront the problems head on, you have a much better chance of making it through the storm. It is not easy. It can be very frightening and unpredictable. But which fate would you prefer: a watery grave or a chance to sail again tomorrow?

Think about that and determine that when the storms in your life come, you will not hide below deck and hope they go away. You will plant yourself at the helm, turn your rudder, confront the waves, and learn your lessons. Seek godly counsel and find out what your Maker is trying to accomplish in your life. Then you will see the amazing view from the wave's crest instead of being crushed in the undertow.

Fill in the Blanks: What is your favorite season and why? _____

_____

Do you find yourself happier that time of year? _____

What special memories do you have of that season? _____

_____

_____

_____

_____

_____

What will you do today to prepare yourself for the storms of life? _____

_____

_____

_____

_____

Run

There was a young man who was very handsome, muscular, and desired by women. As he worked, women would watch. They could not stop imagining what it would be like to be in his arms, held by him, and loved by him.

No, he was not a model, an actor, or musician. He was not rich or powerful. He was a slave. But to the ladies, he was irresistible.

One day while the master was away, the master's wife threw herself on him. Her request came across like a command: "Sleep with me."

Let us assume for a moment that she is fairly attractive. This request/command would be difficult for most men to resist. The master was away. He was a slave with no female companionship to enjoy. He had nothing to offer a woman, so prospects for relationships in his life were ultra-slim.

In that moment, when the demand for sex was made, the woman grabbed the slave's shirt. The path of least resistance would bring temporary pleasure. No one else was around. No one had to know. She was very persuasive. She could make his life miserable if he rejected her.

However, this slave's mind had been made up a long time before this advance. He had strong moral convictions. He knew what he would, and would not do. In that split second of temptation, there was only one option: run.

So, he ran. Her grip on his shirt never loosened, so he left it behind. He ran out of the room, down the hall, and into the slaves' quarters.

When the master returned, the wife was in tears over the rejection. Instead of confessing what she had done, she lied and declared that the slave had forced himself on her. The shirt in her hands was the proof.

The slave was tracked down and thrown into prison for a crime he did not commit. He undoubtedly questioned what was going on.

Why was he stuck there?

How long would he be in prison?

Would he ever be set free?

I am sure there were many days he wondered if he had done the right thing. Knowing the story of this man like I do, I guarantee that he knew he had done what was right.

Running away is the only option for the person desiring to keep their integrity intact. Sure, you can stand there and debate the temptation in your head, weighing the pros and cons of it all. But the simplest solution to temptation is still the best one: run.

Fill in the Blank: "If I was faced with a temptation in an area of my life that I struggle with, I would immediately

_____."

If you wrote anything other than "run", I strongly suggest you study the life of this slave, Joseph, in Genesis chapters thirty through fifty. You will see the same man that ran away from temptation be in the right place at the right time later in life.

Two nations, Israel and Egypt, still exist today because of one decision Joseph made that day to run away from temptation and never look back.

Blue

When you think about the greatest musicians to ever play jazz music, Miles Davis is at the top of a very short list. He is probably the greatest trumpet player since music began being recorded.

In 1959, Davis went to the studio with long-time friend and classical pianist Bill Evans. He and Bill recorded the skeleton forms of songs. Then when the other musicians came in to play, it created greater improvisation for what they would add to the song. That album was titled "Kind of Blue".

According to the Recording Industry Association of America, that is the greatest selling jazz album of all time, certified as quadruple platinum.[1]

It was unanimously voted in as an official national treasure by the United States Congress. This album cemented Miles Davis' legacy and artistry. However, it was not always that way.

For years leading up to that recording, Davis struggled to find bands to join. When he was able to sit in, it was usually short-lived. When he finally got his big shot, he struggled to keep the band together. One of his partners had a mental breakdown on the tour and left Miles stranded in California. There were always conflicts in musical direction, style differences, and personal problems. At one point he nearly had a meltdown when the style that he had made famous, known as "cool jazz", was attributed to other jazz musicians.[2]

Then there was heroin.[3]

It claimed the life of several of his musician friends. Yet he still struggled with the addiction. He went through several periods where he got clean, only to relapse.

It just seemed like he was destined to fail. He could not keep bands together. He could not keep his personal life in check. After fifteen long years of playing in no-name clubs, recording what he could, changing musicians as often as he changed venues, it just seemed like the dream was over.

How close had Miles Davis come to throwing in the towel? How close was he from never setting foot into a studio again?

Thankfully, we will never know. Regardless of the innumerable setbacks he faced, he grabbed his trumpet, called a good friend, and recorded something that has become part of American cultural history.

Fill in the Blanks: Are you close to giving up on your dream? _____

_____

What are the obstacles in your path which overwhelm you with discouragement? _____

_____

_____

You can give up and become one of those washed up musicians of whom no one will ever hear. You can give into the blues. Or you can keep fighting for your dream. You can allow those stumbling blocks to turn into stepping stones and obstacles to turn into opportunities. You can take all those struggles, turn them into a "Kind of Blue," and possibly write your way into history.

Shalom

There once was an old woman who had no children.[1] In her culture, children were considered a gift from God, so if a woman could not have kids, she was considered cursed. A prophet of God came and told her that she would have a child. After the child was born and grew, the boy came home from playing outside complaining of a tremendous headache. Not long after, the boy died. This child – that she did not ask for, but was blessed with – was dead. So she pursued the prophet.

When anyone asked her if something was wrong, her response was "It is well." This phrase, which also means "Everything is alright," is just one word in the original language. It is the Hebrew word *shalom*.

This word also means "peace". However, it is much deeper than that. It means wholeness, completeness, and not lacking any good thing. It means all is well. It means that in your heart and mind, *everything* is all right.

Now, how can a person whose son has just died say, "It is well"? Only a person of deep faith can make such a statement in those kinds of circumstances. Ultimately, it is a person who has resolved in their heart and mind that, despite the desperation of the circumstances, God has the last word on everything.

Such is the story of a man named Horatio Spafford.[2]

He was just a regular American businessman. However, in 1871 the Great Chicago Fire destroyed Spafford's real estate business. His entire life savings was lost.

Two years later, he and his family decided to take a voyage to Europe via ship. He was delayed at the last minute, so his wife and four daughters went on ahead of him. Aboard the S.S. Ville de Havre, their ship sank in the Atlantic Ocean on November 21, 1873 after being hit by another vessel.

When his wife was rescued from the shipwreck, she sent a telegram to him saying, "Saved alone. What shall I do?" Spafford received the telegram and left to meet his wife.

As he sailed across the Atlantic, surely a flood of emotions hit him. He must have likened his life to that of Job, having lost his business, life savings, and his four daughters with only him and his wife to live on in sorrow and pain.

The Captain of the ship told Spafford that they were passing the place of the shipwreck, which had become the tomb for his four little girls. He grabbed a pen and paper and he wrote the words to the song "It Is Well":

When peace, like a river, attendeth my way,
When sorrows like sea billows roll;
Whatever my lot, Thou hast taught me to say,
"It is well, it is well with my soul."

Hopefully, if you ever get severely tested in any area of your life, you have resolved to fill in the blank with, *"shalom,"* knowing that peace, wholeness, and completeness are God's way of ensuring He always has the last word.

Fill in the Blanks: If I ever endured something like these two characters, my first thought would be:

_____

_____

Is that how God would want me to react? _____

_____

_____

Flap

Penguins cannot fly.[1]

Yes, they are birds. Yes, they do have wings. But they do not fly. That is to say, they do not fly in the air. Nonetheless, what they do is pretty amazing!

Their feathers are short and tight against their body to reduce drag unlike most other birds. Their bones are not hollow, therefore they are dense and perfect for diving. They have a higher body mass index which insulates it from the cold. Penguins are designed to be very hydrodynamic, not aerodynamic. Their flight is through the water at amazing speeds and depths. Their soaring is through vast water currents.

However, imagine a penguin whose fascination it is to fly. Though it is physically impossible, this certain penguin dreams of soaring above the icebergs and floating effortlessly hundreds of feet in the air.

Sadly, it will never achieve this dream because it does not have the right tools. The tools it was given are for swimming and not flying. This poor penguin is dreaming of doing something for which it was never made.

I firmly believe that each person is born with God-given talents and abilities. When you operate outside of those gifts, you struggle because you are doing something outside of your talents. You are dreaming of flying when you are built for flapping.

However, when you are operating in the areas for which you are keenly talented, it is as effortless as a penguin in the ocean. You are doing what you were born to do, what you were gifted to do, and what comes perfectly natural for you.

I encourage you to take an inventory of the things in which you are gifted. Start a list of the things you enjoy doing, and the things that come natural for you to do. You may not even enjoy those activities now. But when you find an area you are gifted in, it will bring joy and fulfillment.

Whether it is dance, music, writing, painting, or something else entirely, honor God, the Gift-Giver, and you will see how far that talent can go. Discover the tools that you have been given, sharpen them, and use them. When you do that, you will experience happiness in your life where you are productive, creative, and fulfilled.

Fill in the Blank: What are areas of your life in which you are naturally gifted? _____

_____

_____

_____

_____

_____

Commit to being the best you can in those areas. Surround yourself with people who have the same gift which will help you cultivate yours. You may dream of flying, but you were born to flap. Embrace that and be content with whom you were made to be.

Piano

When Mozart sat down to play the piano, he placed his hands gently about certain notes as he formed chords with his hands. He played artfully and beautifully. He used his skill to create music when there was previously silence. His hands glided up and down in a fluid motion. He added Diminished 7ths and Suspended 4ths for flair and depth to his chords.

From his perspective, he experienced the beauty of it all. But from the perspective of the strings, it was not so beautiful. It was actually painful.

Each note was created when a hammer struck a string. There was no other way to make the sound. The strings must endure moments of pain to create this beautiful music. If the hammer struck the string gently, barely any music was heard. If the hammer struck the string with force, it resonated music loud enough to fill concert halls.

While the pianist sits at the piano, the strings do not question him, "Why did you strike me? What have I done to you? Why is this happening?" Rather, they understand their purpose in this world. Without the hammer striking them, they know that it is impossible for their purpose to ever be realized. They weren't made to sit. They were made to sing.

In your life, have you ever felt like the hammer was pounding on you? Have you ever been in a situation where you felt like you were being beaten over the head? Were you tempted to cry out and question God? Did you wonder why these bad things were happening to a good person?

The fact is we will all experience times of struggle. We will feel like we are being struck with a hammer. Instead of feeling like a nail being driven down into the ground, realize that you are a string.

It is when the hammer strikes you that you make the most beautiful music. The harder the hammer hits, the louder your song becomes. With God's hands on the keys, He knows just how much each string can take to make it fill His concert hall with glorious music.

Fill in the Blank: When you go through times of struggle, you are tempted to react this way:

_____

_____

_____

When you went through that, who did you turn to for help and guidance? _____

_____

Do you feel that they helped you? _____

_____

_____

Who should be your first source for help during times of difficulty? _____GOD_____ (And yes, I filled that blank in for you just to make sure you put the right answer in.)

Resolve to let God do what He wants to do in you. Resolve that no matter how hard the hammer strikes you, you will sing through your storm. The harder you're hit, the louder your song.

Overshadow

The two greatest Generals that fought during World War II were Montgomery and Patton. Very few military historians would dispute that fact. Together, their strategies defeated the Germans and ended the war. Sadly, their time was spent fighting each other almost as much as the Germans. They were fiercely competitive and disliked each other immensely. Each of them wanted to be known as the man that defeated Hitler and singlehandedly ended the war.

This became such a thorn in the side of General Dwight Eisenhower, that the stories written after the war focus a great deal on the tense dynamic between Montgomery and Patton. Their accomplishments were overshadowed only by their arrogance.

There is a difference between confidence and arrogance. I believe this difference is rooted in the heart of a person. If you have accomplished much in your life and are a "subject matter expert", that earns you the right to be confident. However, in your heart, you must always maintain humility.

You must realize that you do not know everything and therefore cannot act like you do. You must always value the opinions of others, even though they may be much less experienced than you. Sometimes, those inexperienced opinions are right.

The arrogant do not listen to anyone but themselves. They love the sound of their own voice. Many times, they are not saying anything significant. They believe that their opinion is the only valid one.

What makes an arrogant person even harder to deal with is when they have position above you. It can be miserable to work for someone who treats you as if you have nothing valuable to offer the company, who finds fault in everything you do, who takes the credit for all your accomplishments, and who lays all the mistakes at your feet.

One day, the story of your life will conclude. Your friends and family will gather in a chapel or at a graveside. They will say their final goodbyes. Prayers will be offered to comfort the grieving. A eulogy will be spoken.

The question is: will all the things you accomplished in your life be overshadowed by your character flaws? Will anyone there that day be tempted to say, "You know, they did so much in their life. But they were the biggest jerk I had ever met. I am glad they are dead."

Hopefully for you and for me, our hearts are filled with humility and no one could ever say something like that about us. Remember the words from James 4:10, "Humble yourselves before the Lord, and he will lift you up."

Fill in the Blank: One of the character flaws I need to be working on is: _____

_____

_____

If you cannot think of any, just ask your friends. If they are *good* friends, they will tell you honestly how you can improve your character, and be a person who is overshadowed by nothing.

Take a moment to create a plan of action to help you overcome the character flaws listed above. What can you do today about them? _____

_____

_____

What is your goal by the end of this week? _____

_____

_____

In a month, how will you make sure you do not regress back into this behavior? _____

_____

_____

A year from now, you want everyone you meet to describe you as: _____

_____

_____

_____

Soap

I once stared at a bar of Ivory soap and wondered, "Can this thing ever get dirty? Can my hands be so filthy that they actually make the soap something different? A sort of half-soap, half-dirt hybrid?"

So far, soap cleans my hands no matter how dirty they are. After my hands are cleaned, I rinse the bar of soap off and it's as if it had never happened. The soap retains its pristine white look.

There are not many things in life that can do this. For instance, if you put dirt in your dinner, it won't take long for your taste buds to find it. The food will not clean the dirt or water it down. Putting dirt in hand lotion will not help maintain the creamy texture. The composition of the lotion will change. Your skin will go from soft to sand-paper in no time.

Soap is self-cleaning. It cannot be tainted by anything you put it up against, at least nothing I have ever encountered. You could probably dip a bar of soap in motor oil, rinse it with water, and it will most likely be glowing white again.

There is only one other thing I have ever come across like soap. It is not something you would expect, but I do have it on good authority that it works the same. This thing with soap-like abilities is a little more abstract than Ivory, Dove or Lever 2000. It is something called *grace*.

One of the early leaders of Christianity told the Church in Rome this truth: "...where sin increased, grace increased all the more..."[1] Grace cannot be tainted by how many sins you commit or how horrible they are. Grace is spiritual soap.

It is the element from God that allows you to rebuff the filthiness of a sinful life. Sin will pollute you. Its ultimate goal is to kill you physically and spiritually. However, grace is there to help you become free and completely clean. It restores your purity.

Many times, we fail to reach for this spiritual soap because we are too ashamed that we need it. We are mortified of what we have done. We have not forgiven ourselves for our mistakes, and we are embarrassed to ask God to forgive us *yet again*. However, grace is the free gift from God to bring us to a right-standing with him. We need it, so we should condition ourselves to reach for it every time it is needed.

You may have allowed some pollution in your life. Face it: we live in a spiritually-polluted world. However, instead of throwing your hands up in the air and choosing not to fight against sin anymore, choose the better path.

Fill in the Blank: "An area of my life that is not clean and in much need of God's soap is _____

_____.

Today, I choose grace, and go from polluted to pure once again."

Laika

As a person who is a motivator, my job is to encourage you to take risks, make progress, and achieve all that God has planned for your life. You might hear some people use the phrases "step out on a limb" or even "go for broke" to try and motivate you out of complacency and lethargy.

However, there is *no substitute* for wisdom in those choices. I am not standing over your shoulder yelling "Do it!" when you stand in Best Buy staring at a gigantic TV that you cannot afford. Any risk or opportunity you take has to be calculated. Without weighing the pros and cons, you neglect wisdom and take an uncalculated risk. Rarely do those work out for the better.

Laika was a female dog, a stray, sent into space by Russia on Sputnik II. Because the mission was rushed by Communist President Nikita Khrushchev to launch on the one-month anniversary of Sputnik I, the designs and plans were severely flawed. Though they did not make it public at the time, the scientists were fairly certain Laika would not survive the return trip. When the satellite burned up on reentry, the government had told people that Laika had been fine and enjoying the view until that point. The truth was far from that. The dog died just a few hours after launch from a combination of heat and panic. It was all because they chose to take an uncalculated risk.

This time it was a dog. In your case, it could be a career opportunity, a relationship, a financial scheme, or something that feels too-good-to-be-true. Though I try to motivate and inspire, I encourage you to *only* take calculated risks. When you do not, the consequences can be catastrophic.

According to the wisest man that ever lived, King Solomon said that only fools despise wisdom and instruction.[1] He also said that wisdom is calling out to anyone who will listen. Maybe when you are staring at that purchase you cannot afford, relationship you should not get into, investment you should not make, and you have an internal gut check... that is probably wisdom calling out to you. The world has enough examples of Laika. You do not want to be another one.

Fill in the Blank: "I have been tempted to rush into a decision regarding _____

_____

_____

but I am going to embrace wisdom, counsel with others, and pray for guidance. I will not take uncalculated risks."

Commit to this, embrace the gut check, and walk out of Best Buy being satisfied with your smaller TV and the wad of cash you just saved yourself.

Pencil

When you were born, your parents hopefully told you that you could be anything you wanted to be. Hopefully, they encouraged your hopes, dreams, and aspirations. As they did, your confidence grew. You realized there was nothing you could not accomplish. As you won awards, received scholarships, and got the pick of the University you would attend, life just seemed to fall into place.

Or maybe that did not happen for you. Maybe you struggled through school, barely got a GPA high enough to get some financial aid, and had to work through college to make up the difference.

Or maybe your parents did not encourage you to attend college. Maybe they did not tell you to dream big. Maybe they told you to lower your standards, and prepare to join the family business. Maybe they said that college was out of reach; that money was so tight, you could not even afford the application fees.

Or maybe you did not have parents. Maybe you were raised by someone other than your true mom or dad. Maybe the word college never came up in conversation at all.

There is great emphasis placed on higher education, stellar work experience, proficient resume' writing, and achieving all that you possibly can in life. We see examples of people who had a great idea and *hit the big time*. We think that we could certainly do that. It is as if we walk around thinking that the whole world exists merely for us.

In the Bible, we are cautioned to not think higher of ourselves than we should.[1] As a friend of mine pointed out, the entire Bible has one main character. That main character is not me or you; it is God.

From cover to cover, the Bible is not a story of my life, my encounters, my prophecies, or my experiences with God. It is about God's encounters with people who have come and gone long before me.

Sometimes, our place in this world is best summed up by this quote from Mother Teresa, "I am a little pencil in the hand of a writing God, who is sending a love letter to the world."[2] Let the word "little" sink in.

Let God use you, but remember that it is His story being told, and not yours.

Fill in the Blank: An area (or areas) of your life that you tend to "think of yourself more highly than you should" is: _____

_____

_____

_____

Resolve to put God in His rightful place. If you boast at all, boast in Him. You are just a little pencil, but be happy to be in His hands.

Dash

A life is measured by the length of years spent on earth. So much so that when you walk around a cemetery, the grave markers typically share very few things. They list the deceased's name, the day they were born and the day they died. In between those two dates hangs a piece of punctuation that most people completely miss. They ignore the dash. This dash between the day a person was born and the day they died sits on the grave marker like an unwritten book.

That dash contains everything about the deceased. It contains their childhood memories, their hopes, dreams, goals, first kisses, first breakups, and first love. It contains their greatest triumphs and their personal tragedies. It hides their mistakes and character flaws. The dash defines the time they spent on this earth.

My mother spent 64 years and 83 days on planet earth before slipping into a coma and dying. Does that time period define her? Surely there was more to her than just as a resident of this planet. And yes, there was so much more to her than that.

She loved her family. She enjoyed making big dinners so we all could get together and share meals. She loved her grandkids. She enjoyed cross-stich. She sang Alto. She was a whiz at Photoshop and just about any other computer program she needed to learn. Even when I was a grown man, she would slip some extra money in my hand and say, "Do not tell your father." She was an amazing woman. The dash does not do her life justice. But at the end of her life, that dash was still chiseled onto her tombstone.

Before letting your head hit the pillow, drifting off into another restless night just to wake up tomorrow and do the routine all over again, ask yourself these questions and *Fill in the Blanks*: What are you doing with your dash?

_____

_____

_____

_____

If that little piece of punctuation will one day define you, then what are you doing to make it meaningful?

_____

_____

_____

_____

Stage

"All the world's a stage, and all the men and women merely players: they have their exits and their entrances; and one man in his time plays many parts, his acts being seven ages." You may have heard the first part, but that is the full quote from Shakespeare's *As You Like It*.[1]

When I was in high school, I was – how shall I put this – awkward. I played soccer, but did not fit in with the jocks. I was in advanced classes, but did not fit in with the brainiacs. I was a photographer for yearbook, but did not fit in with the artistic crowd. I went four years and never really felt accepted by any group. It left me frustrated and isolated.

In the summer before going off to college, I had an epiphany. No one there knew who I was and that was a good thing. I could be whoever I wanted to be. I could portray myself as the popular, talented, funny, athletic, and artistic person that would be widely accepted. I had the opportunity to reinvent myself. Awkwardness, be gone!

I read Shakespeare's quote and this is what it means to me: you can be who you choose to be. You were not born a selfish jerk. You were not born a victim. You were not born popular. You just choose to act that way. At any moment, you can choose to act different and therefore be treated differently. It is how you present yourself to others that determines whether they accept you or reject you.

I am not advocating you change your personality as often as you change clothes. I am not suggesting you placate to people just to get them to like you. What I am saying is that if you don't like who you are, then stop being that person.

If you are tired of feeling sorry for yourself, then quit doing it. If you are tired of being lonely, start going where people are. If you are tired of not having friends, then start being friendly.

Driving through the neighborhood on the way to my house, I will wave at people standing outside along the streets. My children ask, "Do you know them?" I reply, "No, but to have friends, you have to be friendly." I was not always that way. However, I chose to break out of my shell and become the kind of person I always wanted to be. I am never short on having friends nearby.

Fill in the Blank: Areas of your life that you want to change now in order to be whom you have always wanted to be are: _____

_____

_____

If *all the world's a stage*, and you are a player, then you get to determine the script, the setting, the other players, and if it ends up being a tragedy, drama, or comedy. I vote for the latter.

Signet

Prior to the use of a personal signature, a seal was used to authenticate a letter or document. Wax would be melted, poured over the lip of the envelope, and the seal would be placed over the wax to leave an impression. This would harden as it cooled leaving an unmistakable claim to the veracity of the document in hand.

These large and heavy seals gave way to the use of signet rings. A signet ring could be given to each member of the household to show their allegiance and lineage. It showed that they belonged, they had authority, and their words carried the same weight as the giver of the ring.

The woman in the powerfully erotic poem *Song of Solomon* told her lover, "Place me like a seal over your heart, like a seal on your arm..."[1] She wanted everyone to see her love for him. She wanted to be his forever. She wanted him to know that he had claim to her heart. Only he had the authority to unlock the secrets of her love.

The Apostle Paul wrote that God put his seal of ownership on us, putting His Spirit in our hearts as the deposit to guarantee what is coming.[2] Essentially, when we gave our hearts to God, He sealed our heart with His signet ring, which is the Holy Spirit. This seal proclaims that we have willfully chosen to give Him ownership of our lives. Therefore, we carry around our allegiance to Him and His authority in us.

Fill in the Blanks: Do you live your life in such a way that shows this? _____

_____

_____

Are you as passionate about God as the woman in Song of Solomon? _____

Do you declare your allegiance and love for God as she did, without abandon? _____

Or do you hide that seal from everyone because you are afraid of looking like a fanatic? _____

Jesus said, "Whoever disowns me before others, I will disown before my Father in heaven."[3] We would be quick to respond, "I would never disown or deny him!" However, the way we live our lives is a testament to whether that is true or not.

Here are some more *Fill in the Blanks:* Have there been times where your behavior showed you were ashamed to be considered a Christian? _____

Were there occasions when you knew the right thing to do and you chose not to do it? _____

Was there ever a time when you forgot where your allegiance lies? _____

Accept this challenge: live your life in such a way that you are unashamed of the things you claim to believe. Remember that, if you profess yourself to be a Christian, you walk around with the seal of the Holy Spirit on your heart. Your responsibility to Him is your allegiance; His gift to you is His authority.

Ripe

I am sure you have heard the expression "Strike while the iron is hot."[1] The origin of that statement dates back to the late 13th Century when blacksmiths heated up iron to form it into various shapes. Once the iron was hot and malleable, they would pound on it with their hammers to change it into whatever they wanted it to be. If they missed their small window of opportunity and allowed the iron to cool, it would become hard again and they would be unable to shape it.

Another example of this same principle is fruit. When you peruse the produce section at your grocery store, you typically look for fruit that will ripen soon. When fruit is ripe, it reaches the zenith of its flavor. It will never taste better than it does at that moment.

However, another definition of ripe is *almost rotten*. There are very few worse-smelling things than rotten food. The difference between ripe and rotten is a small window of time. If you do not seize that moment, then you will have lost it. There will not be any going back. The fruit will never ripen again.

There are times in our lives where we are presented with a ripe opportunity. We question it. We investigate it. We vacillate. We hesitate. When we do that for too long, what was once ripe and ready to be a fruitful endeavor quickly turns rotten. We missed our chance. We did not *strike while the iron was hot*. All we are left with is a regret of what could have happened.

I bought a bag of candy for my children. My son was quick to point out that there was a contest and we might have the winning ticket. He was so excited to get home and open it. However, I have lost every sweepstakes I have ever entered and was not so optimistic.

I opened the bag to discover that we had the winning ticket inside. The grand prize was $250,000. My heart started pounding. The instructions told us to call a 1-800 number to claim our prize.

The phone number was disconnected. I tried again. Same result. Once more: fast busy signal. I then looked closely at the winning ticket. The contest had expired one month prior. My son was crushed. I was definitely disappointed. He turned to me and said, "Dad, we could have been millionaires!" I did not have the heart to correct him.

This is an example of the iron getting cold. The fruit had turned rotten. I could not have changed my outcome. Yet there are times in our lives where we can. We may have a golden opportunity ahead of us.

If we feel peace about it and have confirmation that it is the right choice, then choose one of two things: wait and let the fruit rot in your hands; or take a big bite of that apple and realize a new day with new challenges and new opportunities.

Fill in the Blank: What is your iron? What is the ripening fruit that is on your horizon? _____

_____

_____

_____

Make your choice quickly. If you do not seize the moment, it may be lost forever.

Spackle

First introduced in the late 1920's by an American company, spackle has become something that most homeowners and handymen use often.[1] Spackle originally exists as a powder and becomes putty once combined with water. It is used to fill holes in the wall in case you were trying to hang curtains with no success, or for a variety of other reasons. The spackle putty can be smoothed, painted, and made to look like the hole never happened.

It is used as a small scale solution as opposed to cutting out the drywall, replacing it, taping it, texturing it, and painting it. That is a lot of trouble to go through if it is a small blemish. Spackle remains quite necessary to keep the house from looking like you are a bad aim with the hammer. However, you as a homeowner must make a mental note of where you spackled. If you put much pressure on that spot, your hand will go right through the wall.

I have come across people who seem to have used spackle for their character. They had a few flaws, but instead of taking the time and hard work to completely repair the holes, they chose the short-term, cost-effective, easily-covered-up solution of "character spackle". Then there are people who have so many character flaws, they have spackled on top of their spackle. If you put too much weight or pressure on them, they will crumble into bits of worthless putty.

We all make mistakes. We all have flaws in our character that we need to work on. My purpose is not about making you feel bad for having temptations. We all have those. Rather, I want you to be aware of how you have dealt with these character flaws.

Fill in the Blank with your answers to these questions: Have you covered up these flaws in hopes they would go away? _____

_____

Have you hidden your problems from people who care about you and can actually help you overcome these struggles? _____

_____

Or have you done the hard work of cutting out the problem area to completely replace it? _____

_____

_____

When the pressure is on, do you think you will stand strong or would you crumble to the ground like dried-out spackle?

_____

_____

_____

Name

Who are you?

Seriously.

Before you start reading off to me your resume' or your Facebook profile's "About Me" section, give that question serious thought. You are defined by someone or something. There are those who live their whole lives in the definition that their parents forced on them. "Well, dad and mom were both doctors, so I guess I should be a doctor too."

There are those who allow themselves to be defined by jobs: I am an analyst... I am a lawyer... I am an accountant... I am a writer. Many times, men fit into this category. It relates to the punishment God gave Adam in the Garden of Eden: You are what you do.[1] Consequently, this is why some men consider suicide when they are not providing for their families. If they are not *doing* something, they don't feel like they are worth anything.

For Eve, her identity was wrapped up in child-bearing.[2] This is why many times a woman who cannot have a child feels like much less of a woman.

My name, Jason, means "healer". My parents chose that name for me because my birth brought healing to my mom's body. But I have not always been a healer. I struggled for many years to control brutal sarcasm that would bring people to tears. I would wound people with my words, mask it with humor, and blame them for being too sensitive for getting their feelings hurt. "I am just being honest," people could often hear me say. But in reality, I was being unnecessarily cruel with my words. I was tearing them down. I was losing friends fast.

I remember being so upset with myself one day that I resolved to change my behavior. And I did. I still have my sense of humor, but I try hard for it not to be at someone else's expense. I am working hard on a daily basis to live up to my name, to let it define me. I want to be a healer, encourager, and motivator. I want people to walk away after talking with me feeling like they are uplifted and inspired… that they feel better about themselves and closer to God.

The 20th century writer and poet Audre Lorde said, "If I didn't define myself for myself, I would be crunched into other people's fantasies for me and eaten alive."[3]

Let's go back to the beginning and *Fill in the Blanks*:
Who are you? _____
What are you allowing to define you?
_____

_____
Is it your job? _____
Is it your children? _____
Are you living up to your name? _____
Or are you allowing your name to be the opposite of who you really need to be? _____

_____
Instead of "Healer," are you "Destroyer"? _____
"Crowned with glory" or "Filled with shame"? _____
"Gift of God" or "Hell on earth"? _____

"What's in a name," you may ask?
Everything.

Regret

As a minister, I have officiated funeral services from the stillborn to the elderly. It is one part of the job that never gets easier. I have stood in front of the flag-draped caskets of soldiers with hundreds of people attending. And I have stood in front of the cardboard casket of an infant with only half a dozen family members at the cemetery. I have even been able to be bed side while one woman took her final breaths. It is an experience that leaves an indelible impression on you.

While dealing with dying people, you have to realize that their time is short. Because of that, they say what is on their minds. They do not have time to sugar-coat things or consider everyone's feelings. They gather the family to the bedside and give their final words. They reflect on how they lived their life. Many times, it is tragically nothing but regret.

One thing I have *never* experienced was a person who said to their family, "You know, I wished I had spent more time at the office. Yeah, I wished I had worked harder on those reports for my boss. I wished I had done some extra work off the clock and skipped a few more family dinners to really get that big promotion." Nope, I have never heard anyone say that.

What you do hear is a helpless person realizing that the most meaningful way they could have spent their time was wasted. They say, "I wished I had spent more time with the family. If only I had not worked so much, I could have saved my marriage. If I had only taken the time to go to my kids' sporting events... that would have shown how much I care about them."

On and on they go. They open their mouths and pour out rivers of regret.

There was one man in history that was a religious zealot.[1] He was so overtaken with his cause that he volunteered to hunt down people of religious sects and cults to kill them. He felt that he was justified to maintain the purity of his own religion. He traveled to many towns to arrest these people and present them before the religious judges to receive their death sentence.

One day while he was executing arrest warrants, he had an encounter with Jesus Christ that literally changed his life forever.[2] Jesus was not pleased with what he had been doing. In that moment, this zealot became a Christian, the very people he had been hunting. He gave his life to a peaceful pursuit of proclaiming the good news about Jesus. This man, known as Saul and later as the Apostle Paul, had a lot of actions in his life to regret.

However, at the end of his life, Paul did not fill his mouth with regrets. Instead he wrote these words: "… The time for my departure is near. I have fought the good fight, I have finished the race, I have kept the faith."[3] When you are on your deathbed, what words will come out of your mouth? _____

_____

_____

_____

If they are regrets of a misspent life, there is plenty of time to change your course. Live like Paul and be able to say that regardless of your past, you chose to live your life with no regrets.

Oak

You probably already knew this, but an acorn is the seed of an oak tree. This little prize of all the squirrels in my yard is something quite amazing. This little nut can take anywhere from 6 months to two years to develop enough to become a prime seed. When it is time, the oak tree just drops it to the ground. The nuts themselves are too heavy to disperse in the air. Gravity usually ensures the base of the oak tree is littered with acorns.

Different types of oak nuts take varying amounts of time to germinate the seed. However, once the seed begins to grow into a sapling, species of oak trees can live from 200 to 1,500 years. All of that is from one acorn.[1]

The relevance of that fact is this: big things have small beginnings. History is filled with movements, revolutions, and life-changing events that all started with a small beginning.

Think back on your life. How many relationships and friendships started over a simple cup of coffee, a quick smile and hello in the stairwell, or a small gesture of kindness? How many songs have been written trying to express the small phrase, "I love you"?

Whether you know it or not, you are planting acorns all around you. You are dropping seeds of either life or death, blessing or cursing. The words of your mouth can plant a healthy oak tree or a bitter wormwood. Which one will grow is determined by what kind of seed you plant.

To take it a different direction, you may have an idea for something. It is something small. It is a seed for which only you can care. You get excited at the thought of something new being created.

I know the feeling all too well. The articles you are reading are my acorns. But it is a lot of hard work to foster the germination. These acorns do not spring into oaks overnight. Quite the contrary. It is easy, *very easy,* to be frustrated, exhausted, and impatient when the little seed does not grow into something huge as quickly as we would like.

When I get impatient and think about quitting, I remember a verse from the Bible tucked away in Zechariah chapter 4 when talking about rebuilding the Temple from its ruins: "Who dares despise the day of small things...?"[2]

Every thousand-year-old oak tree that shelters countless birds and squirrels had its beginning as an acorn dropped on the hard, cold ground. Every single one of them. I believe that God can look at an acorn and see the oak it can become. The task is to discipline ourselves to see with that kind of vision.

Fill in the Blank: What kinds of acorns are you planting? Healthy ones or diseased ones? _____

_____

If they are healthy, then what are you doing to ensure they grow? _____

_____

_____

If you have a God-given dream, then how are you ensuring that the seed does not die? _____

_____

_____

What are you doing to take the acorn and turn it into an oak? _____

_____

_____

_____

To see our oak trees grow and our dreams come true, we start looking around for the miraculous to happen. As one minister said, "We're looking for a move of God, but God is looking for a move of man!"[3] The oak is there. We just need to make sure that the small beginning does not have an abrupt ending.

Fire

I want you to imagine something with me. I want you to imagine that you are standing in your front yard looking directly at your house or apartment. The problem is that flames are engulfing it. But do not worry just yet. Since this is only an exercise, just imagine that everything is frozen in time. Yes, your home will be destroyed. But we are not racing against the clock. Not yet.

I want you to mentally walk through the door of your home. Imagine looking at all of your furniture, clothes, dishes, food, knick-knacks, computers, and televisions. If you can see them in your mind, I want you to know that they will all be lost. But, again I remind you not to worry about it.

As you move from room to room, you will undoubtedly see things you will want to pick up and save. They may be pictures of a loved one who is deceased. It may be your CD collection with rare Jazz music that would take years and thousands of dollars to replace. It could be your computer that contains your life's work. It could be Prada shoes, custom shirts, or a tie collection that is worth more than my annual salary. No matter what "trophies" you have collected over the years, I am telling you now that you are willingly going to let them burn.

I know you think I am crazy. Surely I do not understand the value of all of your stuff. I must not comprehend how rare that guitar is... or the stamp collection... or the wardrobe... or whatever. You are right. I do not know the value of it. But I know the value of something else will far exceed all of that.

Let's back up. You are in the front yard again. And I am there with you. Hi there.

As time unfreezes and you see the flames licking the roof, you are immediately amazed at the force of the fire. In no time, it is destroying everything. You are overwhelmed that all of your valuables are being destroyed so quickly and effortlessly.

In that moment, I turn to you and say one thing that will immediately change your perspective: "Your family is inside." In that moment, will the CDs, TVs, books, computers, guitars, stamps, or clothes matter one bit? I certainly hope not! In a split-second, the words have sunk in and no one could possibly hold you back. You would not hesitate running inside to carry your family out.

So why do most people live their life prizing things that in that split second matter nothing to them? The TV doesn't care that you got sick enough to be hospitalized. The record collection, though extensive and rare, does not care if you cannot pay your bills. It is time to start caring for things that can care for you back. Jesus said, "For where your treasure is, there will your heart be also."[1]

One day my daughter asked me, "Dad, if the house was on fire and you could only get out with what you could carry, what would that be?" Without missing a beat, I said, "My family." If you were asked the same question, with what would you *Fill in the Blank*? _____

_____

_____

_____

Hopefully, what you wrote above is something that is truly worth saving.

Picture

I was talking to a photographer who said, "You know the expression, 'A picture is worth a thousand words'? Well, it seems some pictures that I see people take are barely worth a dozen."[1]

Ponder that thought for a moment.

A photograph captures a moment in time with unique lighting, shadows, contrast, and composition. The word *photograph* means "to write with light." Every photograph is a poem, a story, an epic. However, some photographs are so poorly taken, they are barely a haiku.

Good photographers know their subject. They know the story behind the smile lines, the story behind the architecture, or the story behind what fills their frame. Because they know the stories, they do not just take photographs. They create art. They capture what you and I may never see with our own eyes. We may never travel the world. But we can see the world the way they see it.

An ancient prophet wrote God's words spoken to him: "Before I formed you in the womb, I knew you..."[2] There is no one like you. From your fingerprints to your DNA, you are an original. You may even have an identical twin, yet you are still mysteriously unique.

Because of all that, your life is similar to a photograph. Your life is a story. It is being written by the things you do, the way you live, the convictions you hold, the causes you join, the songs you love, and the relationships you hold dear. A good photograph tells a story. A great photograph has stories written about it.

Fill in the Blank: When you come to the end of your life, will either of those two hold true for you? _____
_____
_____

If not, what do you need to change today to turn your life from a dozen-word thumbnail to a million-word canvas?

_____
_____
_____
_____
_____

Fork

Often in life, people come to a significant crossroads. The path they are on requires them to choose one of two things: get married or stay single; accept the job or keep looking; buy or don't buy; sell or don't sell. We call this event "coming to a fork in the road." In some situations, it is a major event that requires serious consideration. The reality is that it is not really a fork. It's more of a Y.

A "Y" in the road means that you have two choices. One is usually an action: getting married, taking the job, moving out, buying a car, etc. The other road is usually inaction: staying single, staying unemployed, staying in your parent's basement, or not doing something. Some people can agonize over this, but it really comes down to choosing one of two paths.

I was in the kitchen and the expression came to my mind about a fork in the road. None of my forks look like a Y. My forks aren't fancy or expensive. They are just functional. My forks have four prongs.

Sometimes, the path that you are on is not a simple Y anymore. Sometimes, it becomes a true fork where there are many options to choose from. When you stand at a true fork-in-the-road with four possible paths, it can be easy to despair or be lured into inaction.

I think many people choose the path of *least* resistance. When faced with a multi-pronged path, they choose the easier, less risky one. It is the safe option. It provides the maximum amount of security. If that's you, that is just fine. You are safe in the majority. Most people would agree with you that you did the right thing.

However, my life experiences have taught me a different lesson: the path of *least* resistance comes with the least amount of reward. The path of *most* resistance comes with the most rewards and the most fulfillments.

T.S. Eliot said, "Only those who will risk going too far can possibly find out how far one can go."[1] French Author, André Gide wrote, "One doesn't discover new lands without consenting to lose sight, for a very long time, of the shore."[2] I say it is time to take some calculated risks in life. It is time to stop asking "What might have been" and start seeing "What can possibly be." It is time to live and enjoy it. It is time to see how far you can go.

So *Fill in the Blank*: "I have wanted to try this but I have never had the courage to take the risk. So today, I'm going to take steps towards doing

_____

_____

_____

_____

and with God's help, I'm going to do it."

Destiny

Have you ever come across someone who was so gifted at something, you knew what they would end up doing for the rest of their life? A child who can create their own music at the piano... a person who can paint an amazing portrait without ever having lessons... someone who has a gift and you are pretty convinced they will do something amazing with their life?

Do you know anyone that fits into that category? Well, you should, because you fit into that category too. You see, I happen to believe that each and every person is born with a destiny. Now, I do not believe that someone is making all my decisions for me or controlling me. I believe that I still have the freedom to choose what I do with my life. But I believe that I am predisposed to certain things because of these innate gifts inside me.

Case in point: I will never be a dancer. And I will not even bother trying. I already know it is not the life for me. I know my limitations.

However, I am predisposed to being a musician, writer, and public-speaker. I just happen to be gifted in all three of those areas. I enjoy all of them. When I am involved in those activities, I get pleasure. Writing would be work for some people. They might labor over a few paragraphs, but they come very easy for me. It brings me joy and contentment when I operate in my gifts, when I give myself over to my destiny.

You have a destiny. And I am going to step out on a limb a little to say that you will never be fully content with your life until you find what it is, pursue it, and give yourself over to it.

For some people, they were born to dance. Others were born artists, painters, sculptors, actors, photographers, lawyers, analysts, accountants, or whatever. When you do what you were born to do, it is almost like God's universe is in harmony with you. You have accepted your destiny in this life. It is a very beautiful and fulfilling thing.

Before you do anything else, show some gratitude to God who implanted those gifts in you. Then *Fill in the Blank*: If there is one thing that you could do for the rest of your life and it would make you very happy, it would be

_____

_____

_____

_____

_____

Think about it. Then start walking in that direction today. You will not live in regret when you are living in your destiny.

Goldfish

My children returned from a trip to the carnival with plastic bags containing goldfish. I have never had a fish as a pet. I do not have an extra aquarium in the garage, left over fish food, or anything else necessary for giving fishes an at-home habitat. The best I had was a large glass bowl.

I took the kids to the store and bought some goldfish food. Since I did not have a water pump, I changed the water every other day. The three goldfish turned into two. After a week, another fish funeral was performed and only *Beast*, my youngest child's goldfish, remained.

I was in the kitchen by myself one day and just watched the fish. It was completely dependent on me for fresh water and food. Without me, it wouldn't last very long at all. There it was, just swimming in circles. It examined every inch of the dish for an exit.

The words to the Pink Floyd song had suddenly come to life: "We're just two lost souls swimming in a fish bowl year after year. Running over the same old ground; what have we found? The same old fears. Wish you were here."[1]

I pitied the goldfish. I knew that its life expectancy was measured in days, weeks, and possibly months. The most it could ever aspire to was to swim in clean water and have a full belly. In the meantime, its life consisted of swimming in circles, covering the same ground it had been doing for the previous hours and days.

I looked at the goldfish and realized that I know people like *Beast*. I know people who are just going in circles in their lives.

They do not ever experience anything new. They eat the same thing at the same restaurants on the same nights of the week. They cover the same ground, so they usually stumble in the same spots. Like the goldfish, their life consists of obtaining food and shelter, and not really enjoying anything else about their life.

If variety is truly the spice of life, then it's time to set the goldfish free. Whatever your goldfish is... your rut, your routine, your pattern, your *same-old-ground*... it needs to be examined.

If you find yourself making the same mistakes over and over, then at least commit to make new ones! As the author Andy Andrews wrote in his book *The Travelers Gift*, "When I am faced with the choice of doing nothing or doing something, I will always choose to act!"[2]

Fill in the Blank: In your life, your goldfish is:

_____

_____

_____

Choose to do everything you can to get out of the fishbowl and conquer new territory this year. Do not be guilty of inaction. Move, change, adjust, and be free.

Island

I got a dog. Before you ask, "Why in the world did you get a dog?" I'll tell you that I honestly have no idea why. I just did. He was cute. He was playful. He seemed obedient. And he was obedient... when I told him to do something that he already wanted to do.

At the time, I suppose I wanted the loyalty that a good dog can give. I thought it would be a low maintenance relationship. I would pet him, feed him, give him shelter, and a big backyard to play in. In turn, he would obey each and every command that pops in my head... and provide companionship.

Either I was a terrible master or he was a terrible dog because it just did not work out as expected. Probably, it was a mixture of both. After a month or two, I looked him in his big eyes and said, "It's not me; it's you."

The need for companionship, relationships, and community is within us all. The English poet, John Donne, wrote, "No man is an island entire of itself; every man is a piece of the continent, a part of the main..." Elsewhere in the poem, he wrote, "...any man's death diminishes me, because I am involved in mankind."[1]

I attended a church service where the Pastor said, "Life is intended to be lived in community."[2] We are all on this ball of rock and water called Earth together. My actions affect you and your actions affect me. When we experience life's struggles, it is easy for us to withdraw from the fight like a wounded soldier. However, we are called to stand together, to "bear one another's burdens," to stand shoulder-to-shoulder as we go through life.[3]

You may not struggle with this. You may be a social butterfly that makes friends easily and never feels loneliness. Or you may be an island unto yourself because people reject you, ignore you, or feel as if the world would be a better place without you in it.

If that is you, I want John Donne's words to ring in your ears: "…any man's death diminishes me, because I am involved in mankind." A person's death subtracts from mankind. It subtracts what they had to offer. It subtracts the love they gave and the love they received. It denies the world of their contributions.

You are not an island. At worst, you are a peninsula. But you are still connected to this world. Remember that and share your life with this world. There are God-given talents and abilities inside of you just waiting to be shared. Find your *niche* and let the world see God's gift through your life.

Fill in the Blank: What are some things that you enjoy doing? _____

_____

_____

How can you use that thing (or those things) to add value to someone else? _____

_____

_____

_____

_____

_____

Impress

Dale Carnegie once said, "Did you ever see an unhappy horse? Did you ever see a bird that had the blues? One reason why birds and horses are not unhappy is because they are not trying to impress other birds and horses."[1]

Think about how much time you spend weekly trying to impress other people. How many times do you look in the mirror? How long does it take for you to prepare, perfect, and present your image?

When I started out as a minister, I spent serious time thinking about my image. I thought about how a man as young as me would be taken seriously. I was twenty-two, fresh out of college, and trying to find my *persona*.

When I opened my mouth to speak for the very first time in front of all those people, what kind of delivery would it be? How would I dress? What sort of mannerisms would I develop? Who would I become?

To be perfectly honest, I tried for quite some time to fit into the molds of men I admired. It was the most unnatural feeling in the world. I just could not speak or act like them. It felt completely fake.

One day, it dawned on me that I acted differently because I thought differently. I thought differently because I was different. I would never be happy if I kept trying to be something I was not. I would not be content with working so hard to impress others by looking like something familiar. I needed to be true to who God made me to be.

God did not make me as a clone or carbon copy of anyone, so why was I trying to be one? I had made a prison for myself in the form of other people's opinions, acceptance, and approval of my *persona*. I made the prison and was holding myself prisoner.

I decided that it was time for a jail break. I would no longer be held hostage to the opinions of others. They could have them, but they would not define me. I was going to become who I was destined to be. Only then would I truly be and feel free.

Shakespeare wrote, "This above all: to thine own self be true, and it must follow, as the night the day."[2] I am no expert on Elizabethan literature. However, I interpret it to mean that when you are being true to yourself, things just happen naturally. Yes, the night does come. But so does the day. There is nothing like the feeling of living in sunshine.

Fill in the Blank: One area of your life that you have been caught up in impressing others is: _____

_____

_____

Commit to overcoming that need and be true to yourself. You do that, and I will almost guarantee success, freedom, and peace. You will finally be setting the prisoner free.

Marinate

I am not a big fan of solicitors. I do not like people coming to my front door selling me something or standing out front of businesses that I frequent. Walking up to a local grocery store, my children and I saw a group of children selling something that I had no interest in buying. I avoided eye contact entirely. However, my kids did not.

As we got closer to the door, I fixed my gaze straight ahead. Just a couple feet before the automatic doors opened, one of the soliciting children took a step towards me holding out his product. But he said nothing. His mouth was hanging open, but no words came out.

Once inside the store, my son said, "Dad, he was trying to talk to you." To which I replied, "But he didn't *say* anything. 'He who hesitates is lost.'"[1] My children looked at each other, shrugged their shoulders, and followed me through the store.

There are times in your life where you must act. You cannot hesitate. You must decide, because inaction would create even more problems. However, if you find yourself frequently making these quick decisions, you may need to make sure that you are not overly impulsive or a habitual procrastinator.

More often than not, the better course of action is marinating on it. Think about it. Let it stew. Weigh the pros and cons. Research it. Consider all the options. Pray about it. Ask your trusted friends what their opinions are.

Our culture is in love with the "One-Minute Marinade" where we are not willing to really let anything sit for long. However, a good marinade works its way through the meat, changing the flavor of it entirely. It enhances and improves the meat. When the meat is cooked, it is tender, flavorful, and more enjoyable as a result of letting it marinate.

If you are facing a decision that deserves serious consideration, do not bypass this important step. Brainstorm on every possible pro and con of the decision and subsequent consequence. Get a legal pad, draw a line down the middle, pray, and write these thoughts down no matter how outlandish they may seem. Let your friends and family take a look to help you decide.

As King Solomon wrote, "Plans fail for lack of counsel, but with many advisors they succeed."[2] The New Testament writer James exhorted his readers to ask God when they lack wisdom, because God will gladly give plenty to make the right decision.[3]

Fill in the Blank: What decision(s) are you facing in your life where you could use some counsel? _____

_____

_____

_____

_____

The word of the day for you is *Marinate*! You may not have every question answered. But if you are going to take a risk, it is much better if it is calculated and educated than impulsive and foolhardy.

Perspective

The story goes that a husband and wife adopted twin boys.[1] It did not take long for the couple to see dramatic differences between the boys. One of the boys was extremely negative about everything. He was very unhappy and very vocal about it. The other boy was the opposite: his optimism was almost annoying. The couple was at a loss.

They took their problems to a Psychologist who suggested an experiment. Christmas was coming soon. So the couple was to give the most lavish, amazing Christmas gift to the negative son to see if he could find fault with it. Then they were to give the worst possible gift they could imagine to the optimistic son to see if he would still be positive about it.

Christmas morning arrived and the presents were opened. The negative son unwrapped a gift containing car keys to a brand new Ford Mustang GT. The parents sat on the edge of their seat, waiting for his reaction. "WHAT?! You know I hate Fords! This is ridiculous! Don't you know anything about me? This is the worst gift ever!"

Feeling shocked that he could find anything bad with such an expensive gift, the attention turned to the other son. If he could find anything positive in this next present, it would be quite a shock.

The optimist unwrapped the box and everyone was overcome with the smell. He reached into the box and pulled out a brown paper bag full of poop. Without missing a beat, the optimistic son said, "You are not fooling me. Where there is this much poop, there has got to be a pony!"

This story is a humorous way to illustrate that you will typically find what you are looking for. If you think negatively, you will find something wrong in just about any scenario. However, if you choose to always look for the silver lining, you will find it regardless of your circumstances.

Fill in the Blank: What negative circumstances are you facing right now? _____

_____

_____

Has your perspective on these things been positive or negative? _____

_____

What possible "silver lining" can you find in these situations? (You may have to be really creative with this one, but it is worth the time you'll spend.) _____

_____

_____

_____

_____

If you have been fired, this may be life giving you the opportunity to start the career you've always wanted. If you have recently left a relationship, it is your opportunity to reflect on what went right and what went wrong before starting a new relationship.

Optimism is not living in denial. It is choosing the perspective that, though you might be in a storm, sunshine is on the way.

Mirror

Most people I have met fall into one of two categories. They spend an unhealthy amount of time looking at themselves in the mirror, or they rarely look at themselves at all. Regardless of which of those is you, I want you to think about some things the next time you stand there.

Much of what the world thinks about you is reflected in that mirror image. It is sad really, that we allow so much of our self-esteem to come from external sources. We become defined by our jobs, our friends, our music, our hobbies, and so many other things.

A mirror image is a reflection. When you look at yourself, you see all the things that are wrong. The reality is that this is just your interpretation of the image. The mirror is not judging you. It is not declaring you are unfit for public exposure. It is not telling you that you are too fat, too hairy, too bald, too skinny, or too anything. It is just a reflection.

Before you put too much stock on your interpretation of that mirror image, remember the prayer of a Warrior-Poet: "… and I praise you [God] because of the wonderful way you created me. Everything you do is marvelous! Of this, I have no doubt."[1] There may be things about you that you would gladly change if you had the money. But you only think that way because you are judging yourself against some else's standard.

Case in point: I think that children with Down's syndrome are some of the most beautiful kids on the planet. Yes, they have a physical abnormality. But their happy and joyful spirit on the inside radiates to the outside. They love life! They play hard! They laugh often! They find joy in the simplest of things!

Fill in the Blanks: If you look yourself up and down in the mirror, are you happy with what you see? _____

_____

_____

If you could change something, what would that be? _____

_____

_____

Why would you want to change it? _____

_____

_____

Do you think that you will be happier or more accepted by others? _____

_____

_____

Do you need that kind of approval to feel good about yourself? _____

_____

_____

The next time you look in the mirror and do not like what you see, ask yourself this question: "Whose standards am I comparing myself to? Hollywood's or God's?" Pray about that and start to see yourself as God sees you: wonderfully made.

Swim

I read a story about a 6-year-old girl who was playing in the snow with her family nearby.[1] She lost her footing and fell into the freezing, fast-moving river. Her father began running alongside the river, but could not keep up with how fast it was sweeping her away.

Search teams came out and eventually found three items of clothing she had been wearing. A helicopter with thermal imaging made several passes, but came up with nothing. Eventually, the search was suspended because the weather endangered the search teams. They accepted the fact that the child was lost and may never be found.

I am sure panic overcame the parents as they saw their little girl being rushed away in the current. Fear and horror gripped their hearts and minds. It is hard to know what you would do in that situation. It's just not a situation you imagine yourself ever being in.

But as I read the story, I almost felt my heart shaking on the inside of my chest. I have three children. I remind them frequently that there is nothing that I would not do to protect them. My responsibility as their father is to create and maintain a safe environment. If anything jeopardizes that, then it will be dealt with swiftly and decisively.

Do you know why that father had a hard time keeping up with his child in the river? He was running alongside it. I want you to go ahead and make up your mind that you would do exactly what I would do in that situation. Do not run. Swim! The old proverb is true, "He who hesitates is lost."[2]

Your child is floating away. This is a life and death decision. In a split-second, your action will determine whether your child lives of dies. If you run, it dies. If you swim, you may be able to save your child.

Now you might think, "We both could die!" You would be right. That is a high possibility. But consider this: if my child and I were going to die, I would much rather them be wrapped up in my arms, than floating away all alone.

Before you ever get in a life and death moment, especially with a child or loved one's life on the line, make your decision right now. Swim! If you do not, you will live everyday asking yourself, "What if?" For me, I would rather die trying to save my child, than to live with the regret that I never jumped in the water.

Fill in the Blank: Have you ever (or do you know someone who has) been faced with a life or death situation before? _____

_____

How did you (or they) get through it? _____

_____

_____

Did you (they) sit on the sidelines and wait for it to sort itself out or did you (they) act when the crisis presented itself? _____

_____

_____

If you were faced with an emergency situation now, how would you react? _____

_____

_____

_____

Original

In my all-time favorite movie, *Amadeus*, which is based on the life and work of Wolfgang Amadeus Mozart, one of his fellow composers was shocked to learn that Mozart never made copies of his work. When he was shown page after page of staff, each one he held in his hand was penned by Mozart himself. Each sheet was an original, with no corrections or hesitations in the writing. The music flowed naturally out of him and there was not a single mistake in any of his work.

Has anyone ever said to you, "When God made you, He broke the mold"? Well, that is quite true. There is not another person on this planet just like you. You are, for lack of a better term, an original.

So let me ask you, why do you spend the rest of your natural life trying not to be an original? Why do you spend your life trying to fit into a culture and a system? You join political parties, social organizations, book clubs, bowling leagues, bands, gyms, and so many other things that you fill your calendar with all the ways you try to *belong*. You willfully choose to make yourself a cog in a machine.

What you do not realize is this: the machine is changing you. It is molding you into another likeness. It is cramming your personality, talents, skills, and abilities into a box. It will not let those unique things about you be seen by the world. It is forcing you to become like them, dress like them, spend money like them, idolize the things they idolize, etc. The minister and author, John Mason, titled his 1993 book, "You're Born an Original, Don't Die a Copy."[1]

One of the greatest leaders in the early years of the Christian faith wrote a letter to a church in the highlands of modern-day Turkey, which was then called Galatia. Towards the end of his letter, he challenged the Christians not to compare themselves against one another to see who was better or worse. He wrote, "We have far more interesting things to do with our lives. Each of us is an original."[2]

Right after the Apostle Paul wrote that, he then said to the Galatians, "Live creatively, friends."[3] Do not be boring with your life. Live it creatively. Do not accept the world's way of living as the *right way*. Look at your life from a different perspective, from your Creator's perspective. Each of us is an original, with no hesitations from God in the way we were created. Our life flowed naturally out of Him.

Fill in the Blank: Some ways you can act like more of an original and start living creatively today are _____

_____

_____

_____

Do not just talk about it. Start doing it.
"Live creatively, friends."[4]

Shadow

Putting kids to bed is no easy task. There is brushing teeth, brushing hair, getting on the pajamas, bedtime stories, bedtime prayers, tucking in, goodnight kisses... the list grows longer and longer. Then there are phantom ailments. "I need a cough drop." "I forgot to get a drink of water." "You hugged Sissy longer than you hugged me." Seriously?

When they all get settled, I make sure the nightlight is on. I start to back my way out of the room, saying "I love you. Good night and go to sleep." The peace and quiet does not take long. Invariably, a child will cry out for something. Back into the rooms I go, with a little less patience than when I was in the last time. The more I am called back in, the less patience I bring with me.

One of my children became very concerned about the number of shadows in their room. "That one looks like a monster! And that one looks like an alien!" I try to reason with them: "Children, NASA has scoured the Solar System looking for alien life and they have come up empty handed. It is very doubtful that it would appear in your room... at bed time!" But children do not want logic, reason, and science lessons. They want comfort.

When the look on my son's face was of genuine concern, I imparted this truth to them: "You see a shadow because you are focusing on the wrong thing. The shadow only exists because there is light. The light bounces off things in the room. Those shadows form shapes that might make us a little afraid. But do not focus on the shadows. They cannot hurt you at all. Focus on the light. The light reveals the truth that those things that we are most afraid are really nothing at all."

As I was sharing this with my kids, I started to realize its truth resonating in my heart and mind. I have worried myself from time to time with shades and shadows. Spiritually speaking, the farther I was from the Light, the longer those shadows draped themselves over me. However, the closer I got to the Light, the smaller the shadows became as they faded into nothingness.

Fill in the Blank: How many times have you distanced yourself from Christ and been worried about the shadow filling your mind? _____

_____

_____

Is fear an everyday emotion for you? _____

_____

_____

Are you honestly where you need to be with God right now in this very moment? _____

_____

_____

Are you stronger spiritually than you've ever been? _____

_____

_____

Does the enemy of your soul consider you a serious threat?

_____

_____

_____

When you run from the light, all you can see is shadow and fear. Turn around, face it, and draw near. You will see that there is nothing to ever be afraid of when you are standing in the light.

Thistle

The legend goes that an invading army was sneaking up on the Scots one night.[1] One of the invaders stepped barefoot on a thistle, cried out in pain, and warned the Scots of the invasion. The thistle has been the national symbol of Scotland from the 1200's.

If you have ever tried to pick a thistle, you would know that gloves are not optional. The name of the plant alone warns you that you should just keep on moving. When it is not in bloom, the thistle is a nasty little thing. It usually has a large green bulb at the end with long needles just daring you to come close.

The stem has much shorter and smaller needles, but they are no less frustrating. However, when the bulb opens up, an amazing explosion of color catches your attention. Though the name does not lend itself to the idea, thistles are in fact beautiful.

The English Author, Samuel Johnson, once wrote, "Nothing will ever be attempted if all possible objections must first be overcome."[2] I think he was saying that great things in your life are like thistles. They are covered in very good reasons to just keep moving. However, if you are willing to wait for it, make the proper preparations – like gloves and pruning shears – then the beauty is worth the effort.

Maybe you are already thinking about the thistle in your life: that frustrating thing that just eludes you. You want it. But every time you reach for it, you get hurt. You know that it is something you were meant to experience. That is why you keep coming back to it, like you are circling the block to see if the flower has bloomed yet.

When you think about this thing, be it a career change, relationship, opportunity of a lifetime, or whatever... you just have a feeling that it is eventually intertwined with your life. That is why you keep coming back to it. That is why you are willing to put up with the pain, rejection, and frustration. When you think of it, you get the feeling that it was something for which you were born. You have a sense of destiny about it.

I am not going to tell you what to do. It may not be the right time just yet. But I will tell you what I did. Metaphorically as well as literally, I grabbed the thistle with both hands. I twisted it and turned it until the needles broke into my skin and caused quite a bit of pain.

However, I refused to let it go. My thistle might not have meant anything to anyone else, but it meant everything to me. When I held it in my hand, the pain I went through to get it made the beauty so much more fulfilling.

Think about it for a moment. As you have read this chapter about thistles – something that has eluded you – has your mind already gone to something specific? *Fill in the Blank:* My thistle is: _____

_____

_____

_____

and I am willing to put up with the pain to enjoy its beauty for the rest of my life.

Tailspin

I have always been fascinated with airplanes. I wanted to build model ones when I was little. I wanted to be an Air Force pilot and get to sit in the jets. I wanted a cool nickname like "Maverick" or "Wolfman".

The main problem with that dream is that I truly hate flying in airplanes. I would rather drive than fly. I know there are many people who are the exact opposite of me. But I get *very* spiritual when I have to fly. I feel very vulnerable and out of control when flying in the air at 600 mph.

If you have ever seen stunt airplanes do tricks in the air, it is really amazing. One thing that pilots will do is climb really high, stall the engine and turn the tail rudder, or yaw, so that the plane corkscrews down to the earth. This is also called a tailspin. I am sure this move gets the pilot's heart pounding.

Sometimes in life, we stall out. We stall in a relationship. We stall at our job. We stop moving forward. In that moment, we must make a critical decision. Do we crank our engines back up, or do we turn a different direction.

When you are stalled and turn off course, you enter a tailspin in your life. You will feel completely out of control. In the moment that you needed to "hit the gas", you were indecisive; or you chose inaction; or you chose a foolish one.

When Moses, one of the greatest leaders Israel ever had, was coming to the end of his life, he gave a series of instructions to the people. He had passed on the commands that God had given him and he said in Deuteronomy 28:14, "Do not turn aside from any of the commands I give you today, to the right or to the left…"

As you plummet and feel the full force of the tailspin breeding stress in your life, you have one more chance for survival. Pilots call it "stick into the spin." It means instead of trying to fight it or letting go of all control, you actually turn into the direction you are spinning. You realize that you are headed down, but you know down is the only way up. Sometimes people hit rock bottom. But the great thing about that is there's nowhere to go from there but up.

Hopefully you are not in a tailspin. Hopefully you cannot relate to this at all. But if you are, realize these two important things: you are not alone and you will recover.

Fill in the Blank: The area (or areas) of your life that you are most likely to get stalled and go into a tailspin is/are: _____

_____

_____

_____

Identify that, determine to keep your foot on the gas and do not get off course. Straight ahead is your destination and you want to get there in good shape.

Toilet

I know what you are thinking. "This seriously cannot be the real topic." Oh, but it is!

The chain-pull indoor toilet was invented in England in the 1880's. About ten years later, flush toilets were introduced. Though there are variations on toilets across the world including urinals, squatters, port-a-potties, and others, the civilized world is accustomed to, and dependent on a toilet being close by. When you go to a mall or amusement park, sometimes the first thing that is located on the map is the nearest restroom... especially if you are a parent!

When I was a child, my parents took me to a shoe store. I told my dad that I desperately needed to use the restroom. When my dad asked the employee were the bathroom was, the employee replied, "We do not have a restroom."

Knowing that was a lie, my dad turned to me and said, "Ok, son. I guess you will just have to pee on the floor." I looked at my dad in disbelief. Suddenly, the employee said, "Don't do that! I will take him to the bathroom." We went through a series of double-doors and – wouldn't you know it – a toilet magically appeared even though he said they did not have one.

Imagine with me for a moment. If your company decided they were converting the bathroom into a storage room, that restrooms would no longer be offered, and you would simply have to hold it until you got home... Or if they forced everyone to go back to the days of the chamber pot or outhouse, how long would it take before there was a revolution on your hands at the office? In our culture, the toilet is absolutely indispensable. We have come to appreciate its usefulness in times of desperation.

Now put this in a spiritual context. God wanted the people of Israel to build a Tabernacle, a house of worship, which could be moved as they travelled through the land. In order for it to be acceptable, God gave very specific requirements for the construction. God told Moses that He would impart special wisdom to skilled craftsmen to make the things that He wanted for the Tabernacle. They were going to make things that were truly one-of-a-kind, indispensable, and amazing.

I know this seems like a rare occurrence, but I think God looks for people who will commit their craft to Him, whatever it is. I think He is looking for people that will use their minds to dream, their eyes to see, their ears to hear, and their hands to create something uniquely amazing.

Fill in the Blank: What is your "toilet"? What is something that you can contribute to the world that is indispensable, that there would be a revolution on our hands if someone tried to take it away from us? _____

_____

_____

What is an area of your life that you can partner with God in to see some amazing things come of it? _____

_____

What talents can you turn over to God to let Him pour His creativity into you? _____

_____

_____

_____

Think about it and then do what the Apostle Paul said, "Live creatively, friends."[1]

Wonder

When I was a child, the holidays were always a magical time. As I have grown up, I have noticed that Christmas just does not seem the same anymore.

Each morning, I bundled up with about six layers before heading out the door for school. I had a yellow knit hat that had a plastic Big Bird attached at the top. When I got outside, a crisp breeze would bite at my face. It felt like Christmas.

At school, we had plays, decorations, Christmas tree cookies, and construction-paper snowflakes. In the evenings, every house would be lit up with bright lights, wreaths, and lawn decorations. From the street, you could see each family's Christmas tree. There was no escaping it. It looked like Christmas.

Around the neighborhood, people were lighting their fireplaces with treated wood that had such a great smell to it. I would walk in the front door of my house and smell apples and cinnamon. Spices, food, hot apple cider... It smelled like Christmas.

Each and every day just added more and more anticipation. Sure, I was excited for the winter break from school. But I was more excited about Christmas coming. Every kid in the class was sure they knew what their parents were getting them. In my young mind, this was the best time of the whole year.

As a grown-up, I have noticed that something has changed in me. Like many people, I work right up to Christmas day. I avoid the stores and do my Christmas shopping online because I loathe standing in line. For me, Christmas had lost the magic. It had lost the wonder.

Let me rephrase: Christmas has not lost anything. But I did. I lost that expectation and the excitement of the season. From the Christmas play at church, to the big family dinner, it started feeling like any other holiday. I started to ask myself when this changed for me.

When you are a child, you believe in the Easter Bunny, Tooth Fairy, Santa Clause, and all sorts of magical creatures. Children easily believe in things they have never seen because they were born with and maintain a sense of wonder in their heart. They have great faith.

At some point, those mythical beings are exposed as frauds. Consequently, the holidays stop feeling so special. They become just another day where the banks, stores, and offices are closed. Just another day to buy something that is not in the budget. Just another day of lost productivity. Just another day facing a family member that rubs you the wrong way.

But I have made up my mind. I am restoring the wonder. I want to embrace the amazing, distinctive, and extraordinary moments that make up this day. From the sights and sounds, to the tastes and smells… I want to not just experience it. I want to savor it.

Fill in the Blank: Do you feel like Christmas has turned into more "hustle and bustle" than a season of wonder? _____

_____

What can you do to restore that sense of wonder in your life? _____

_____

_____

Let this season go from wonder-less to wonder-full.

Epilogue

First of all, thank you dear reader. Thank you for acquiring this book legally (I hope). Thank you for reading it. I sincerely hope that there is at least one chapter that spoke to you in a profound way.

The first edition of Volume 1 represents a year of work in brainstorming, writing, editing, revising, website creating, Facebook and Twitter page designing, as well as so much more. The revised and expanded edition you have just completed represents over six months of additional work between me and my editor. We tried to refine and perfect each chapter as much as possible to give you an even greater product than the first time around.

Also, I stuck with saying that this is "Volume 1" because I have written more chapters, and have many more ideas jotted down to provide more volumes to this brand.

I greatly appreciate your feedback and your stories as to how these chapters have provided encouragement. I recommend you share your feedback on the Amazon.com page for the book so others can see the benefit of reading this short volume of powerful stories.

Please stay in touch with us via our Facebook, Twitter, and website as we will post updates of the work on Volume 2. The links are in the "About the Author" section at the very end.

Finally, I would like to offer a pastoral prayer for you from Numbers 6:24-26: "The LORD bless you and keep you; the LORD make His face shine on you and be gracious to you; the LORD turn His face toward you and give you peace."

Chapter Notes

Gold
   1. Isaiah 48:10, NIV.
Exit
   1. Jonah 1:3, NIV.
Finish
   1. http://sports.espn.go.com/espn/espn25/story?page=moments/94
   2. http://joeldurston.wordpress.com/tag/derek-redmond/
Pink
   1. http://www.marketplace.org/topics/world/tracing-origin-pink-slip
   2. http://www.empower-yourself-with-color-psychology.com/color-pink.html
Fruit
   1. Genesis 1:22, 28; 8:17; 9:1, 7; 35:11; Jeremiah 23:3; Ezekiel 36:11
Blue
   1. Ted Giola, *The Jazz Standards: A Guide to the Repertoire* (New York: Oxford University Press, 2012), 11.
   2. I hate citing Wikipedia, but they do have a very thorough article on Miles Davis here: http://en.wikipedia.org/wiki/Miles_Davis.
   3. http://www.biography.com/people/miles-davis-9267992. Also see this article for even more info: http://www.milesdavis.com/us/biography
Shalom
   1. This story comes from 2 Kings 4:8-37.
   2. http://www.loc.gov/exhibits/americancolony/amcolony-family.html
Flap
   1. Look up "penguin facts" on the Internet for lots of fascinating things about these unique birds.
Soap
   1. Romans 5:20, NIV.
Laika
   1. Proverbs 1:7, NIV.
Pencil
   1. Romans 12:3, NIV.
   2. http://www.goodreads.com/quotes/30608-i-m-a-little-pencil-in-the-hand-of-a-writing

Stage
1. The full text of "As You Like It" can be found here: http://shakespeare.mit.edu/asyoulikeit/full.html. For Shakespeare's complete works, see this link: http://shakespeare.mit.edu/

Signet
1. Song of Solomon (or Song of Songs) 8:6, NIV.
2. 2 Corinthians 1:22; 5:5, NIV.
3. Matthew 10:33, NIV.

Ripe
1. http://www.phrases.org.uk/meanings/strike-while-the-iron-is-hot.html

Spackle
1. http://dictionary.reference.com/browse/spackle

Name
1. Genesis 3:17-19, NIV.
2. Genesis 3:16, NIV.
3. http://hellopoetry.com/-audre-lorde/quotes/

Regret
1. Acts 8:1-3, NIV.
2. Acts 9:1-8, NIV.
3. 2 Timothy 4:6-7, NIV.

Oak
1. http://www.buzzle.com/articles/facts-about-oak-trees.html
2. Zechariah 4:10, NIV.
3. This quote is credited to Rev. Willie George of "The Church on the Move" in Tulsa, Oklahoma.

Fire
1. Matthew 6:21, NIV.

Picture
1. Emile Browne is the photographer on which this article is based. Check him out at www.Facebook.com/emilecbrowne.
2. Jeremiah 1:5, NIV.

Fork
1. http://www.goodreads.com/quotes/9819-only-those-who-will-risk-going-too-far-can-possibly
2. André Gide, *Les Faux Monnayeurs*(1925). The original quote is in French: "On ne découvre pas de terre nouvelle sans consentir à perdre de vue, d'abord et longtemps, tout rivage."

Goldfish
1. Pink Floyd's "Wish You Were Here" was originally released in 1975 on the album bearing the same name.

2. http://www.andyandrews.com/downloads/print/AA_SevenDec
isions.pdf.

Island
1. http://www.poemhunter.com/poem/no-man-is-an-island/
2. Pastor Sam Rudd of Life Church in Katy, Texas.
3. Galatians 6:2, ESV.

Impress
1. http://quotationsbook.com/quote/18285/
2. http://shakespeare.mit.edu/hamlet/hamlet.1.3.html

Marinate
1. This quote is based on a statement from Joseph Addison's play
   Cato from 1712 in which a character states, "The woman that
   deliberates is lost." See http://www.yourdictionary.com/he-
   who-hesitates-is-lost.
2. Proverbs 15:22, NIV.
3. James 1:5, NIV.

Perspective
1. A version of this story was often told by President Ronald
   Reagan. See
   http://www.heritage.org/about/press/remembering-ronald-
   reagan

Mirror
1. Psalm 139:14, CEV.

Swim
1. http://usnews.nbcnews.com/_news/2012/01/24/10222696-a-
   second-of-inattention-icy-river-sweeps-girl-6-away-from-
   father?lite
2. See reference 1 above in the chapter "Marinate."

Original
1. Mason, John. *You're Born an Original, Don't Die a Copy.*
   Sevierville, TN: Insight Publishing Group, 1993.
2. Galatians 5:25, The Message.
3. Galatians 6:1, The Message.
4. Ibid.

Thistle
1. http://www.visitscotland.com/en-us/about/arts-
   culture/uniquely-scottish/thistle
2. http://www.brainyquote.com/quotes/quotes/s/samueljohn1220
   57.html

Toilet
1. Galatians 6:1, The Message.

ABOUT THE AUTHOR

Jason M. Frazier is a husband, a father, a son, a brother, and a follower of Jesus Christ. He is a former Officer in the US Army Reserves.

He earned his undergraduate degree from Southwestern Assemblies of God University, his Master of Arts in Religion from Liberty University, and has returned to Southwestern to complete his Doctorate (D.Min.).

He plays four instruments, has written over thirty poems, and actively follows Scottish and English Football.

To book the author for a speaking engagement or for general information, e-mail **FillintheBlankBook@gmail.com**

Stay up-to-date with Fill In The Blank by visiting us on our website, as well as Facebook and Twitter

www.FillintheBlank.me
www.Facebook.com/Fill.In.The.Blank.Podcasts
www.twitter.com/FillTheBlank_me

Download the mobile app at **fillintheblank.mobapp.at**

Portrait courtesy of Emile C. Browne Photography
www.Facebook.com/EmileCBrowne

My Notes

Made in the USA
Lexington, KY
16 December 2018